DYING FOR A DRINK

DISCARDED
From the Nashville Public
Library

DYING FOR A DRINK

A Pastor and a Physician
Talk about Alcoholism

Alexander DeJong *and* Martin Doot

as told to Cecilia Hofmann

William B. Eerdmans Publishing Company
Grand Rapids, Michigan / Cambridge, U.K.

CRC Publications
Grand Rapids, Michigan

Published jointly 1999 by
Wm. B. Eerdmans Publishing Co.
255 Jefferson Ave. S.E., Grand Rapids, Michigan 49503 /
P.O. Box 163, Cambridge CB3 9PU U.K.
and by
CRC Publications
2850 Kalamazoo Ave. S.E., Grand Rapids, Michigan 49560

03 02 01 00 99   7 6 5 4 3 2

Library of Congress Cataloging-in-Publication Data

DeJong, Alexander C., and Martin Doot
Dying for a drink: a pastor and a physician talk about alcoholism /
Alexander DeJong and Martin Doot; as told to Cecilia Hofmann.
        p.   cm.
Eerdmans ISBN 0-8028-4622-X (pbk. alk. paper)
CRC Publications ISBN 1-56212-397-1 (pbk. alk. paper)
1. Alcoholism — Religious aspects — Christianity.
2. Clergy — Alcohol use — United States.
3. Alcoholism — United States — Physiological aspects.
4. Alcoholics — Rehabilitation — United States — Family relationships.
5. Alcoholics — Rehabilitation — United States.
6. DeJong, Alexander C.
I. Doot, Martin.   II. Hofmann, Cecilia, 1947-   .   III. Title.
        BV4596.A48D45   1999
    362.292 — dc21   98-49965
                                        CIP

Contents

Foreword

This is a very personal little book, and I am a little person who feels impelled to begin in the first person. This is also a book about a phrase that appears on page 1: "full disclosure." So I will make a full disclosure and say that one of the co-authors, Dr. Martin Doot, was at one time our family physician. While I have seldom seen him in recent years, I have vivid recall of our relationship and from it draw confidence in his work and words. (He offered excellent care and empathic counsel when my first wife and our family were dealing with her terminal cancer — the best test I know.)

I was also for a time on the board of MacNeal Memorial Hospital, where the other co-author, Pastor DeJong, began his treatment and recovery. So I have confidence in this particular facility, although both of the authors and I are aware that such treatment could have been undertaken at any number of other places.

End of my "full disclosure." The authors also make their joint acknowledgment to Cecilia Hofmann, disclosing that she, as they say, "wove our collective stories into a readable text." Whoever did what, this book did turn out to be more than readable. So now let me become impersonal, neutral, fair-minded, and objective to say this: After reading the galleys, I left my study for wife Harriet's studio and mentioned that, while I own a decent library of books on addiction and have weekly access to many more, this succinct address to the issue is the most helpful I've yet seen, and I consider it far more important than its modest scope would suggest.

Suppose you have not read the publisher's copy on the back cover. Suppose you have not peeked at what follows this foreword. Suppose that you are therefore coming "cold" to the ensuing pages. Then let me set up a situation for a sure-fire way to avoid the disease of alcoholism.

First, be sure to have dedicated, faithful, Christian parents. Let the father be a minister in a quite conservative denomination, where God's law and God's love are taken equally seriously. Become a minister yourself, so you have all the spiritual resources you need to ward off the threat of bad habits, addictions, and diseases. Develop a fulfilling ministry to which you bring talents that help you counsel people with addiction problems and win their confidence.

Enrich this set of premises by marrying well, choosing, as in this case, a gifted, theologically informed teacher. Raise a family in which the dual voices of law and love, backed by God's Word and enlivened in daily life, get their hearing. Let the spouse continue to be a partner in work and in leisure. Develop habits that reinforce the marriage — for example, the custom of winding down in easy chairs and comparing notes at the end of the day.

Since you may want insight into health problems, why not have children and see that all three of them become physicians? Develop friendships with physicians, and a deep friendship with one who can look you in the eye and level with you.

With all these elements in place, you are all set to be addiction free, leading what at least in this respect is a blameless, shameless life.

And then wake up one day to recognize, upon the doctor's urging, that none of the defenses helped. You have to acknowledge that you are a hopeless alcoholic. No, not hopeless. Dr. Doot is going to tell you, Reverend DeJong, that you have a chronic but treatable disease. You surrender and begin taking tentative steps toward recovery to face what here is called a "desperate" situation.

If this were only a narrative of how someone got into this circumstance, the book would be engrossing but not helpful. Instead it does help, thanks to the information Dr. Doot provides on up-to-the-minute understandings of how alcohol affects brain chemistry, what kinds of therapies are available, and the importance of spiritual counsel. It also helps to have the personal accounts of both Reverend DeJong and his wife, including their reflections on the resources of faith. I'll get offstage very soon now, so they can do what this foreword says they will do.

What I like about the book — besides its narratives, current data, questions for discussion, and further suggestions — is its moral point. The authors recognize that alcoholism is a disease and never treat it as a mere sign of human weakness or sin about which to be ashamed. Yet they also recognize that the individual, especially if supported by community — such as Alcoholics Anonymous and church-based support groups — can take responsibility and must do so.

José Ortega y Gasset's life motto was "I am I and my circumstances." The genetic determinist says, "I am my circumstances. I cannot help it that I was born with a kind of brain chemistry that makes me vulnerable to alcohol and a candidate for alcoholism." The self-helping egotist says, "I am I." She takes on herself the whole responsibility and believes that she can transcend her genetic programming, life experiences, and habits. No, "I am I and my circumstances" sets up the dialectic that informs this book.

Words on pages cannot effect what a look in the eye or the experience of living with an addicted person can do: bring to life all the passion and fury, the frustration and disappointment that alcoholism elicits from the individual who would be good and do good. But this book comes very close to doing so. In the process it makes clear that gaining ground against alcoholism and becoming and staying dry is a tremendous challenge — physically, emotionally, psychologically, spiritually. With helpers like Dr. Doot and Reverend DeJong and AA and clinics and medicines and God and friends, at least one does not face the challenge alone.

Martin E. Marty

Preface

It has been sixteen years since I was asked to write the preface for Alexander C. DeJong's first book about his recovery from alcoholism. That was a special moment in my personal and professional life. Alex was the father of my best friend, pastor of my parents' church, former president of the college I attended, and the first professional I was privileged to treat. I was reminded of my own feelings about the opportunity to treat his illness while speaking at the annual conference on Dental Well-being in Chicago. I was presenting the results of the research on outcomes of treating health professionals for addiction. Alex came to mind as I described the process of intervention, assessment, treatment, and monitoring of the recovery of health professionals. I spoke of the fear, the shame, the questions about recovery, the reentry into the profession, and the effects on the family.

I traveled from the conference to Green Lake, Wisconsin. My family and I had been invited to the DeJongs' cottage on the lake. In the early morning, while having my quiet time on their deck, Alex and I reflected on the experience. I knew he had a drinking problem long before he was ready to receive help for it. How hard it was to wait when I knew excellent help was available. I also knew a lot could be done to prepare for the time when he might be ready. His family could be educated. I could provide him with the book he requested "to help someone in his church who may have a drinking problem." I smiled as I sent him John Keller's book, *Ministering to Alcoholics*. I could learn how to treat his illness. I could work with a trusted team of professionals who had the skills to assess problems like his and treat the physical, mental, emotional, social, and spiritual aspects of the disease. And I could pray.

Then one Monday morning, he called. He said he was sitting at home with his Bible, John's book, and his bottle of booze in front of him. He wanted help, but he was afraid. What would people think? Would it destroy his ministry? He had taught me about faith in God; I asked him to trust himself to my care. He accepted my advice and was ready to get help. He has been sober ever since. But that was just the beginning of the story. Since his recovery, Alex has gone on to help many other Christians struggling with the disease of alcoholism. I have gone on to make helping professionals my life's vocation.

But why another book? Alex said that he still gets request for the information in his first book about alcoholism, which is no longer available. His family never got the opportunity to tell what it was like for them to experience his illness, the fear of his getting help, and then going public about his illness. I never had the opportunity to tell what treatment for his illness was like and how professional help for his illness has improved since the early 1980s. And so much more is known about alcoholism now than at that time.

Preface

Our vision, born that summer morning in August of 1997, was to write again about the experience, the illness, the treatment, and the hope available to others struggling with the disease. The vision would not have become a reality without the courage of Alex's wife and children, who were willing to tell their part of the story. It would have stayed a dream without the organization, research, and writing done by Cecilia Hofmann, who wove our collective stories into a readable text. We would not have been able to have her expert help without the financial contributions of Alex's three sons, who saw this project as an investment in reenergizing their elderly father's ministry. We would not have the excellent illustrations of alcohol's effects on the brain without the artistry of Alex's talented grandson, Chad DeJong.

Our motivation in sharing this with you is to give you both current information and genuine hope. Alcoholism is a treatable disease with an excellent prognosis when the proper help is given. Lack of knowledge keeps some from knowing how to offer help; stigma still keeps individuals and families from seeking help. We hope this book will break these bonds and set people free to embrace healing for themselves and others.

Martin Doot

Walking on Water
Pastor DeJong Reveals His Problem

I dreaded the moment my parish members would learn of my *problem*. "After all," I thought, "aren't clergy persons supposed to walk on water — and do so without making a splash?" But I had to tell them the truth. They had to know why I was not preaching that Sunday morning. They had to know why I was a patient at MacNeal Memorial Hospital. They had to know that my *problem* was alcoholism. In my terror, I would have much preferred to be suffering from appendicitis, a disorder that raises genuine concerns, or even cancer, a disease that elicits sincere sympathy and powerful prayer. To be afflicted with alcoholism somehow seemed unpardonable, especially for a clergyman.

But with firm resolve I set my feet on the path of full disclosure. Despite the uncertainty of where this path would lead, I committed myself to composing a note that would be read to the congregation of the Kedvale Avenue Christian Reformed Church in Oak Lawn, Illinois. With support from my wife, Joanne, and my physician, Dr. Martin Doot, I planned and carefully crafted the message that would change my life's course.

1

The public reading of the note was likewise carried out with cautious concern. Aside from my family members and one church elder, no one knew about the announcement which would follow the benediction closing that Sunday service. Even Pastor Juan Boonstra, who led the church service that day, was unaware of the startling ending this worship would take. Joanne, my personal Rock of Gibraltar, sat through the service alongside David and Gwen and Dick and Patty, two of our adult sons and their wives. Gwen, herself a "P.K." — preacher's kid, that is — had wisely urged Joanne and the others to be present at this important time.

At the appointed moment the designated church elder positioned himself strategically on the platform behind the pulpit. On my behalf, he read

> *I am in MacNeal Memorial Hospital in Berwyn, Illinois. With full acceptance that I have the disease of alcoholism, I voluntarily submitted myself to the total program of this alcohol treatment center. This program is directed by a staff of competent doctors, counselors, and nurses. My family joins me in requesting your prayers that our Savior will place His healing hand on my life.*

The worshippers sounded a synchronous gasp, and subsequent conversations in the narthex and in the parking lot reflected a mixture of confusion and concern. Parishioners enveloped my family members — there were embraces, tears, and many questions. Can we send cards? Can we visit? Do you need anything, Joanne? What kind of treatment will Alex get? How does he feel now? How long will the treatment take?

2

As the initial commotion subsided, the congregation began to leave. They needed to go home, to absorb the shocking news, and to better understand the path ahead. For some, darker questions came to mind. Why did our pastor choose this route of full disclosure? Will he be terminated? Wouldn't it have been easier to slip away secretly for treatment at that famous center in Minnesota?

The indisputable fact was that the congregation members and I had embarked on a remarkable journey together, a trip on which we would all learn much about the causes of and treatments for alcoholism. None of us would remain unchanged by this experience.

There were distinct stages in my journey with alcoholism. At first I was unaware of and denied having any problem. Gradually I recognized that I was drinking too much, and I felt a sense of failure and personal disappointment. As my dependence on alcohol increased, I struggled to maintain an outward appearance of composure in front of my family, friends, and colleagues. Eventually I surrendered control to the substance itself.

I had always been able to "hold my liquor," so I never felt drunk with a capital "D." I just felt good. Because of the good feeling I got from drinking, I didn't want to quit permanently; so I devised an exercise to prove to myself that I was not an alcoholic. I decided to stop drinking temporarily, and for one full year I drank no alcohol. So there it was — proof positive that I wasn't hooked.

But my final fall was unexpectedly swift. In August of my year of abstinence, Joanne and I traveled from our home near Chicago to an idyllic vacation spot on the coast of Maine. To our great surprise and delight, we discovered that some longtime friends were visiting the same resort. We had dinner together and toasted each other with serendipitous pleasure, little suspecting that this celebration would rekindle a growing addiction.

There were warning signs on the way down. These were the times when dancing on whiskey felt as good as walking on water. Although I carefully avoided weekend drinking to maintain my pulpit persona, there were a few occasions when my drinking habit interfered with my professional responsibilities.

Once, following a funeral service, I went to "lunch" with the soloist. When one drink led to another, I lost track of time, and I was late for the children's catechism class I taught after school. My ever-alert wife, who was a teacher at the school alongside the church, noticed the children playing outside longer than usual. She quickly stepped in to conduct the class — an indication that the good Lord was watching over me even then.

On more than one occasion, I took the telephone receiver off the hook and drank my allotted amount of alcohol, comfortable knowing that I would not slur my speech or forget about a possible incoming phone message. I had carefully hidden my supply behind my books on the shelf in my study.

These experiences might have served to alert me that the forces of alcohol addiction were beginning to take hold of an otherwise logical and committed professional. Unfortunately, I overlooked the cues in this stage of denial.

By April of the following year, I was drinking more heavily, and I was more tightly fettered than ever before. In the end, my frequent daytime routine included purchasing a half-pint of whiskey and driving four blocks to Mount Greenwood Cemetery. There I would drink and converse with the Lithuanian portraits of the deceased who grinned from the headstones. The surroundings were familiar and safe, and my companions were cordial, if not wholly convivial. In the afternoon I'd drink to unwind from my so-called busy day, and at night I'd drink after everyone had gone to bed.

In truth, these peculiar patterns actually defined the essence of alcoholism. I drank increasing amounts of alcohol with increasing frequency. I drank alone to hide my drinking from a disapproving wife and unsuspecting colleagues. And I was so controlled by alcohol that I failed to recognize the total insanity of my behavior.

When I first admitted to myself that I had an alcohol problem, I frequently asked, *Who and what can I blame? Am I completely responsible for my own demise? Can my problem be attributed to bad genes? Am I a victim of a stress-filled lifestyle?* I eventually recognized that there may have been a partial *yes* in the answer to each of these questions.

Yes, I did choose to drink alcohol. We were not teetotalers in my family. My father, who had also been a clergyman, often received bottles of "holiday cheer" from his parishioners. It was their way of celebrating a year of good health and blessings or of acknowledging God's guidance through a year of bad health and bad circumstances. When I became a pastor, parishioners still gave me these "gifts" in a kind and convivial spirit. Like my father, I accepted and drank this "good" whiskey in the spirit of congeniality and gratitude that it represented.

So, did I blame my parishioners for my drinking? Of course not. Did I blame myself? Yes, but in those early days I

5

drank only in moderation. If I had known where those jovial toasts would lead, I might have made different decisions. But how was I to know?

It is now well understood that alcoholism runs in families, so I also had my parents to blame. In my case, there was no doubt that my alcoholic predecessors were on my mother's side of the family. Uncle Al, my mother's younger brother, suffered from alcoholism all of his adult life, a life shortened by the toll of his drinking. While I was growing up, Uncle Al's problem caused much whispering in our home. Once, my parents even contrived a plan to divert him from drinking by settling him on a chicken farm in rural Michigan. They thought they could cure Al by separating him from his booze, filling his lungs with fresh country air, and keeping him exceedingly busy with farm chores. But Al thought otherwise. So strong was his craving for alcohol that he resourcefully "drank" the chicken farm. He routinely stuffed a chicken into a paper bag, headed for town, and swapped the chicken for a bottle of whiskey. Dear Uncle Al — it's a sad legacy he left behind.

Did my stressful lifestyle also deserve some blame? This was, in fact, a justification I used for relaxing with Joanne at the end of our separate workdays. Our shared cocktail hour before dinner was an opportunity to swap stories. Joanne always had a tale about a clever, amusing, or mischievous student, and I always tried one-upmanship with a story about a clever, amusing, or mischievous parishioner or colleague. We also had tough days. Both students and parishioners had problems and concerns, and we each wanted to shepherd our respective charges through their troubled times. By evening, Joanne and I sometimes had heavy burdens to unload, and our wind-down sessions seemed a sensible way to cope.

I thus blamed my drinking problem on myself, my relatives, my work, and all of society. But such blame provided only short-lived solace. In the end, the origin of the problem really didn't matter.

The bare truth was that I had a severe problem, and I was desperate to deal with it. Ultimately I learned that the best way to overcome an addiction is to seek appropriate medical care. Fortunately for me, this care was available when I was ready to admit that I needed help. I called Dr. Martin Doot, a close friend and colleague of our oldest son, Alex. Dr. Doot is an addiction specialist.

QUESTIONS TO CONSIDER

1. Why is it so difficult for a person to admit having a drinking problem?
2. How can family, friends, and church members encourage alcoholics to be open and honest about their addiction?
3. Where should an alcoholic go to get help?
4. What should you do if someone confides in you that he or she is struggling with a drinking problem?
5. Whether you're an alcoholic or not, give examples from your own life where you've used denial or blaming strategies to deal with a problem. Did those strategies work?

Families Get Alcoholism Too
Words from the Drinker's Spouse

Dr. Doot offers this preface to the story:

The problem with alcoholism is that it doesn't just affect individuals — it affects entire families. According to a recent medical report, persons with alcoholism and their families need supportive health care at rates two to three times higher than comparable families of similar size and age ranges. Another study found that children in families with an alcoholic parent are admitted to hospitals 25 percent more often than other children.

Joanne, Pastor DeJong's wife, was so deeply affected by the painful experience of her husband's alcoholism that at first she did not want to relive this tragic time in her family's life by writing about it. But eventually she agreed to share her feelings in order to help those with similar problems. Through her strong faith, her persistent love, and her determined spirit to do what was right, Joanne helped her husband recover and avoid relapse. Her poignant story, however, reveals that in the beginning she experienced deep feelings of fear, uncertainty, and loneliness. If you or your family are suffering from alcoholism, you will no doubt relate to some of the events and emotions recalled by the wife of a person addicted to alcohol.

Joanne's Story

During the last few months before Alex went into treatment for alcoholism, I lived with a great deal of raw fear. Our home was the church parsonage; our incomes came from the congregation and from the associated Christian school where I served as librarian and teacher of English and Bible. Our livelihood was totally dependent on the Christian community in which we lived. I was afraid we would lose it all when our supporters learned that Alex had fallen prey to alcoholism.

I would say to Alex, "Surely you're not going to throw everything away for a bottle of booze." To me, it was inconceivable that he was powerless over alcohol. I noticed that he never drank when he was scheduled to preach or speak publicly, an indication to me that he retained a measure of control. How could he exert control during periods requiring his best efforts, and totally relinquish control during less demanding times? What was control, anyhow? Was it merely a matter of deliberate choice of behavior? If one could control drinking on certain days, why not on others? I did not understand that alcoholism, as a progressive disease, would gradually diminish such hard-won control.

I have learned that many families get stuck at this point. Their alcoholic has given countless indications that he or she has the disease, and they have struggled together to control or stop the drinking. Although all efforts have failed, there is something — perhaps fear of public opinion — that keeps families from actively encouraging the alcoholic to seek treatment.

There are delays, procrastination, and excuses. "This is just a bad phase." "It will get better." "He [or she] will soon

9

see the light." Then we analyze what may be causing the drinking problem and try to control the contributing factors. We think that perhaps we should change certain family routines or schedules, or that we should avoid friends who set bad examples.

Eventually we discover that most attempts at home cures are unsuccessful. The reality is that families with alcoholism lead roller-coaster lives that rise with hope and fall with fear and anxiety. Families need to realize that most persons with alcoholism can overcome their problem, but only with professional treatment or through membership in Alcoholics Anonymous. Procrastination allows problem drinking to continue and to intensify.

When we were considering treatment for Alex, I too had to surrender, but I didn't do so immediately. I did not understand addiction. To me the answer seemed simple: quit drinking — end of story. I thought that Alex, in his position as a respected pastor, could not admit to being an alcoholic. The idea was unthinkable to me. I even tried to promote a stay at the Hazelden alcohol clinic in Minnesota, hoping others would see it as a "vacation" and nothing more. I thought Alex should get "the cure" and be done with the whole bitter problem. How little I understood at that time!

As someone in a leadership position in the Christian community, I felt a duty to live an exemplary life. This had never before seemed a burden, but now I found myself pretending to be a person I was not. I wanted the road to sobriety to involve something less than full disclosure.

In this situation I felt torn because I wanted Alex to be healed, but I didn't like the way healing would happen. My sons — far more knowledgeable and objective about alcoholism than I — were joyful when Alex admitted himself into treatment and told his congregation about it. I myself would have preferred a less disruptive course. After our personal bomb exploded, a church elder asked me, "Couldn't it have been done differently?" The elder meant well, but he shared my discomfort with going public. I know that many families faced with a similar dilemma can appreciate my ambivalence about treatment that is publicly acknowledged.

I, like many others, had not yet encountered one of the fundamental statements of AA's *Big Book*, "We go to any lengths." This means we must be willing to surrender whatever it takes to achieve sobriety, even if we are misunderstood or condemned by persons around us. The truth is that the disease of alcoholism is not like appendicitis. Alcoholism carries with it a stigma of moral weakness and self-defeat. The alcoholic is not without blame, and family members and friends always wonder what they could have done to prevent the condition.

I was aware that I could learn about alcoholism through Al-Anon, a group that offers support to relatives and friends of alcoholics. But I could not let myself go to the meetings — attending them would mean I had admitted to myself and others that a drinking problem existed in our family. Instead, I slipped into the safety and anonymity of the public library and read all I could find on the subject of alcoholism. As I read story after story about living with an alcoholic, a pattern emerged. The details of each story differed only in the amount of havoc wreaked on the lives of those involved. Inevitably, the alcoholic sank deeper and deeper into addiction before seeking help.

I could not believe that Alex would follow this standard

path. Surely his deep understanding of human behavior and his high level of spirituality would preserve him from public disgrace. I admonished myself for entertaining the prospect of such a devastating outcome. But the days became more unpredictable and difficult as Alex's drinking intensified.

At this point I decided that all liquor should be banished from our home. In the evening, Alex and I unwound with Diet Coke instead of alcoholic drinks. But that didn't work. We no longer communicated. I sensed that Alex was drinking during the daytime when I was away at school, but he denied my accusations. The wall of secrecy that separated us grew wider and taller.

All trust and security were gone. I lived each day with the certainty that some disaster would occur — a car accident, a gross social error, a financial fiasco. So I worried constantly, double-checked everything, searched for liquor bottles, and rarely committed to advance invitations. I became a prevaricator, making a range of excuses. "Alex isn't here right now," or "Alex has a flu bug today," or "Alex is in a meeting."

The Christian school where I taught seemed an island of sanity where children, fellow teachers, and library orderliness filled hours that were predictable and secure. I loved teaching and could easily turn off my thoughts about the turmoil at home between the hours of eight and four. Sunday also provided respite. Always an inspiring preacher, Alex never lost his ability to preach the Word with enthusiasm and strength. He continued to maintain the respect and affection of his parishioners. He advised many about their personal problems, even giving guidance to those who had alcohol problems. Each Sunday, I was reassured that everything would work out, that much of my anxiety was self-imposed.

But Monday follows Sunday, and the week never passed without a measure of alcohol-induced conflict. Fortunately, the congregation was filled with kind and understanding people who were apparently unaware of the turmoil in the parsonage. If there were whispers, we didn't hear them.

Eventually Alex walked a tightrope of satisfying his need for alcohol and meeting his many pastoral duties. Though he was a caring person who long maintained dedication to and control over his activities, alcohol began to dictate his schedule. It drove him home to a hidden bottle when he might have lingered at a meeting or stayed with a troubled church member. Although I desperately wanted healing for my husband, I wondered whether his absence from his job for substance-abuse therapy would unravel his parishioners' faith and trust. Would all the good he had done over so many years be reduced to dishonor? Above all, I wanted God's name to be honored through us. And I could not bear to bring disgrace on the church or on one of God's servants.

Although I tenaciously adhered to hope for home remedies, I finally realized that Alex could not recover without professional help. Our longtime family friend, Dr. Martin Doot, quietly but persistently reminded me that alcohol addiction *could* and *should* be treated. Our sons, all three physicians, underscored the need for medical intervention and treatment. They knew the disease of alcoholism — its signs, its symptoms, and its treatment. Alex, my oldest son, prodded me: "Quit worrying about the people, Mom. They'll come around. And if they don't, we'll deal with that problem when it's time. It's Dad's life we're talking about — he has a terminal disease." He explained that Dad would need initial treatment as a hospital inpatient, along with at least several months of follow-up visits three times a week. And he prodded harder when he insisted, "And you've got to get involved, Mom. He'll never make it without your support."

I had finally pushed myself through denial and ambivalence about Alex's problem with alcoholism. I was now ready to follow the prescriptions of Dr. Doot and my sons. But I didn't know how the necessary intervention would happen. Again I was advised by my family medical team: we could do nothing until Alex was ready for the treatment. So we waited until the right time came.

With members of a fourth-grade class at the Christian school as unwitting agents of action, the right time arrived unexpectedly. The teacher of the class asked me if Pastor Alex would show slides and talk to the class about our earlier visit to the Holy Land. By then I knew not to commit or cover for Alex, so I replied, "Why don't you call him? I don't know his schedule right now." Alex agreed amicably, and I held my breath and prayed that all would go well.

The presentation was good. Alex always loved children, and he spared no charm when he was with them. But on that day, something in their innocence, their honesty, and their carefree outlook got to him. He later confided that he had wondered to himself, "Why can't I feel like that?" I also learned that on his way home he stopped at the liquor store for his daily half-pint. At home he sank into the recliner, sipped from the familiar bottle, and stared at the pages of *Ministering to Alcoholics*, a book by John E. Keller that Dr. Doot had given him.

Then he acted on a sudden urge and telephoned Dr. Doot. My husband knew Marty as our son Alex's best friend when the two were growing up. He also knew that Dr. Doot was now a physician who specialized in diseases of addiction at MacNeal Memorial Hospital in Berwyn, Illinois. Dr. Doot was available. He asked if Alex was able to drive to his office in Berwyn. They made plans to meet there immediately.

What Can You Do When You Have a Family Member or Friend with Alcoholism?

It is imperative to realize that you *cannot* "fix" the problem of alcoholism yourself. Your alcoholic family member or friend must be ready to get the treatment that he or she needs. You generally cannot force the issue until the time for treatment is right. This is the reason that appropriate medically directed intervention is necessary.

It is wise and essential to remain supportive through those stages when an alcoholic remains unready for help. This position will prepare you to suggest active treatment when the alcoholic is ready to accept it. While it is frustrating to wait, there are many things that you can do while waiting:

- Learn about the disease of alcoholism, and help your alcoholic friend or family member understand that alcoholism is a treatable disease.
- Reassure the person that alcoholism is not his or her fault and therefore not a shameful disease.
- Make it clear that people with alcohol-related problems, like others, are responsible for their personal health.
- Protect your own physical and mental health, as well as that of other family members or affected friends.

15

A support group like Al-Anon can be very helpful. It is often heartening to know that you are not alone in facing the problems of alcoholism in your family or among friends. Alateen is another support group that helps teenagers face the complications of adolescence with the confounding burden of an alcoholic parent. Such groups can provide valuable resources and strategies for coping with alcoholics. Support services for alcoholism can be located by contacting Alcoholics Anonymous or other local organizations listed in the Yellow Pages under "Alcoholism Treatment" or a similar heading.

Above all, remain hopeful and persevere. Alcoholism is a treatable disease, and your family member or friend can eventually return to healthful living. Trust in the Lord that there is hope and help for everyone.

QUESTIONS TO CONSIDER

1. What were the effects of Alex's alcoholism on his spouse and his family?
2. What kept Joanne from encouraging Alex to get help? Are those valid reasons?
3. How can we create an environment that encourages families of alcoholics to find help and support?
4. Where should a spouse or a family member of an alcoholic look for help?
5. What can family members do when the alcoholic is not yet ready to seek treatment?
6. What should you do if someone tells you that one of their loved ones has a serious drinking problem?

Finally Ready for Treatment
Dr. Doot Explains How It Happens

I f you believe in divine encounters, I'd say mine was knowing the DeJong family from the time I was a child — Alex DeJong Jr. was always my best friend. As a longtime friend of the family and as a medical professional working in the field of addiction, I was aware of Pastor DeJong's alcoholism all along.

I helped Alex's wife, Joanne, and their three sons — Alex Jr., Dick, and David — understand that alcoholism is a chronic but treatable disease. Like other chronic diseases such as diabetes and asthma, alcoholism has specific symptoms and follows a predictable course. In addition to producing serious physical effects, alcoholism also overtakes mental functioning to attack the psychological, social, and spiritual well-being of its victims. It is sobering to recognize that untreated alcoholism is a progressive disease that can lead to death.

By deeply influencing normal brain functions, the disease itself causes individuals to deny the reality that they have lost control over their drinking. So — unlike most other diseases — alcoholism cannot always be treated immediately.

For treatment to be effective, alcoholics must reach a point when they are ready to face their addiction to alcohol. Individuals who drink heavily but remain in *denial* will not yet admit to their drinking problem. *Ambivalent* drinkers are those who may recognize their problem on some occasions, but otherwise rationalize that there is no problem. Only those who are *ready to take action* will agree to getting the needed treatment for alcoholism. Although I prayed repeatedly for an opportunity to treat Alex, he was unwilling to recognize his addiction to alcohol for well over a year.

We now realize that more than half of all persons newly diagnosed with alcoholism deny or are ambivalent about their drinking problem. In the past, many doctors and families dealt with this situation exactly as the alcoholic did — they put on their blinders and overlooked the problem and its treatment. By contrast, other doctors firmly prescribed a course of unsought treatment, and families helped force-feed this undesired course to the alcoholic like a plateful of green vegetables.

We now understand that neither approach is correct. It is inappropriate to overlook an alcohol problem once it is evident. It is likewise ineffective to argue with an alcoholic about his or her problem or force him or her into treatment; such actions only lower the likelihood that he or she will accept the needed care. The preferred approach for both doctors and families is to provide persistent reminders about care and treatment until the person with alcoholism is ready for treatment.

Finding the right physician to shepherd an alcoholic and his or her family members into and through treatment is an important early step in the recovery process. A knowledgeable doctor is one who fully understands the disease of alcoholism — its physical and psychological effects, its impact on entire families, and its proper treatment, which will help in-sure full recovery and prevention of relapse. For help in find-ing a physician who is experienced in treating addictions, contact the national office for the American Society of Addic-tion Medicine in Maryland (phone 301-656-3920 or http://www.asam.org).

The support of a knowledgeable physician can be helpful in many ways. First, the doctor can make or confirm a diag-nosis of alcoholism by taking a careful history, using labora-tory tests and physical findings. Sometimes a person with an alcohol-related problem will face the reality of the illness when confronted with direct evidence such as alcohol-induced damage to the liver or stomach. The doctor may also identify other health problems, such as high blood pressure, that can be treated. When persons who have become ad-dicted to alcohol experience early improvements in their gen-eral health, they may be encouraged to seek treatment for their alcoholism.

Since caring physicians can suggest return office visits, they will have repeated opportunities to reinforce their desire to help their patients with alcoholism treatment. Return vis-its also provide doctors experienced in recognizing the stages of alcoholism a chance to periodically assess their patients' readiness for treatment.

Consider the experience of Clarence, a person who regu-larly visited physicians for treatment of his gastritis and high blood pressure. When Clarence came to my partner for treat-ment, he recognized his alcoholism and confronted him with the diagnosis. Clarence later recalled, "I finally listened when he told me I had an illness that could be treated. His confi-dence and concern convinced me to try to get better."

When Clarence asked me why none of the physicians who treated him earlier had asked him about his drinking, I admitted that, unfortunately, not all doctors are fully prepared to recognize and treat alcoholism. Some physicians were trained in times or places where screening for alcohol-related problems was not emphasized. However, all physicians who practice according to current standards of medical care should routinely check for and treat the common conditions of alcohol abuse and alcohol dependence.

Such well-trained physicians and their professional staff members can also provide encouragement and support for family and friends, often called co-alcoholics, who are frightened and confused by the havoc alcoholism causes. In the case of the DeJong family, I helped them learn about the disease of alcoholism. I offered advice about coping with the uncertainties of day-to-day living. I helped them learn how to survive — but not facilitate — the drinking behaviors. I reassured them that treatment programs were available and effective. And I alerted them to the signs of readiness for treatment.

Eventually all of us were ready for Alex to enter active treatment, but we all knew that it would be necessary to wait until he was ready too. When I heard Alex's voice on the telephone that morning in April of 1978, I realized that he finally sounded ready for treatment. In carefully measured tones, I encouraged him to enter the alcoholic treatment center at MacNeal Memorial Hospital to get help from its team of professionals. I held my breath as I waited for his answer. He quietly agreed to meet me at the hospital. This was the God-given opportunity that we had long awaited.

20

If ignoring or covering up the alcoholic's problem isn't the answer, and forcing the alcoholic into treatment isn't going to work either, what should professionals and family members do to help?

How can codependents "survive — but not facilitate — the drinking behaviors"?

Steps toward Treatment

Treatment for each person with alcoholism takes a customized course, but the essential tools that were available to Alex are available to everyone. Also, there are some remarkable new tools that have been introduced in the twenty years since Alex was diagnosed and treated.

Individuals enter treatment at different stages of their illness, and they respond differently to various forms of therapy, so each may require a unique strategy for recovery. The important thing to remember is that there is some form of help for every alcoholic person who needs it. In the sections that follow, I briefly describe the usual approaches to treating alcoholism. This section is intended to offer help and hope for individuals with alcoholism and for their supportive family members and friends.

The Initial Evaluation
of Physical and Mental Status

For nearly all alcoholics entering treatment, the initial step is a complete evaluation of the severity of their illness. In Alex's case, he was interviewed and examined by a physician at the treatment center. Additional interviews were conducted by nurses and addiction counselors. The aim of these sessions was to determine the degree of his physical dependence on alcohol. By reviewing Alex's health history, the results of his physical examination, and the results of laboratory tests, it was possible to determine the degree of his addiction to alcohol.

The immediate aim of the detailed examination was to determine whether Alex would require medication to prevent convulsions or other discomforts when he stopped drinking. Fortunately, Alex's physical withdrawal symptoms were not severe; he needed medication only to help him rest soundly during his first few nights in the unfamiliar setting of the hospital treatment center.

The professional team also looked for signs and symptoms of other health problems related to alcoholism. Complete treatment of all aspects of health increases the likelihood of full recovery from alcoholism. Here are some of the questions that a concerned treatment professional will ask:

- Have any bodily systems been affected by the excessive alcohol consumption? For example, has the patient experienced stomach inflammation or liver damage?
- Are there any underlying illnesses that might be worsened by drinking? For example, was the patient's high blood pressure aggravated by drinking? Once the patient has stopped drinking, it may be necessary to reduce the dosage of medication used for treatment of this condition.
- Does the patient have any underlying emotional and/or behavioral illnesses? Problems such as anxiety or de-

pression are treatable, but when untreated, such conditions may encourage continued drinking.

A Plan to Move Forward

After a patient has been fully examined and interviewed, a team of doctors, nurses, and addiction counselors can recommend a plan of care. In making this plan, the treatment team will take into account the patient's motivations for treatment, likelihood for relapse, and amount of support he or she can expect from family and friends. A patient is usually guided into undertaking three basic types of therapy: (1) participating in individual or small-group therapy led by an addiction counselor, (2) participating in twelve-step therapy for behavioral change through Alcoholics Anonymous (AA), and (3) taking action to prevent relapse. In addition, the treatment plan may recommend that the patient use a medication that curbs the craving for alcohol — a newly available drug that promotes recovery without relapse.

Group Therapy

Group therapy is led by an addiction counselor. These therapy sessions provide a time and a place where each person with alcoholism reveals how drinking has affected his or her life. With the assistance of the group leader and fellow participants, each alcoholic is encouraged to accept his or her condition and surrender to God in order to overcome this devastating disease.

> What does it mean that the alcoholic must "surrender
> to God" in order to overcome alcoholism?

Acceptance is essential to moving forward. Persons who want to recover must first accept the fact that they suffer from the chronic and progressive disease of alcoholism. This disease is characterized by a complete loss of control over drinking alcohol. They must also face the hard reality that there is no cure for alcoholism, so the only viable alternative is complete abstinence from drinking, one day at a time — forever.

Surrender is the next active step. People whose willpower has been defeated by alcoholism need hope for lasting sobriety; such hope comes from faith and surrender to the "Higher Power" of God and His grace.

This key step toward recovery comes with recognizing that the fellowship of AA has helped millions of alcoholics gain and sustain their sobriety. AA offers all participants great hope for successful recovery.

It was in group therapy that Alex's experience took an unexpected twist. As a clergy person, Alex had no difficulty quietly praying to the invisible spirit of the Lord. Likewise, he fully understood the importance of "spilling one's guts" — this practice was the basis of endless counseling sessions he had conducted for troubled parishioners. But when it came to openly discussing his own private thoughts about his drinking problem, he had a difficult time. With considerable prodding from addiction counselors, AA group leaders, and fellow AA members, Alex became increasingly able to talk about his troubles. He learned that being open was not easy, but was an invaluable tool for recovery. And as his recovery proceeded, he

24

shared his small daily triumphs with people who could fully appreciate the importance of each step forward.

Group therapy also provides a time and place to learn about alcoholism as a disease. Recovering alcoholics can learn how drinking can affect thought processes, emotional well-being, personal behavior, and social interactions. Through counseling and discussion, group members can realize how the power of denial blocks recovery. Participants also come to recognize links between their drinking behaviors and a wide range of negative consequences — physical, social, legal, financial, and spiritual.

It is surprising to discover how much some people are willing to lose before they recognize that alcoholism is responsible for their losses. Some never understand. Charles, for example, was a prosperous Colorado businessman who lived with his wife and two daughters in a gorgeous house that had a breathtaking view of the Rocky Mountains. When his alcohol-driven behavior became intolerable, his wife ousted him from their home and divorced him. His daughters lost affection for him, and his business partner bought him out. He squandered the quarter-million-dollar business proceeds on a mistress who in turn provided little more than a warm bed and a place to drink. After repeated drunk-driving violations, he was sent to jail. He was unable to attend his own daughter's wedding — not only because he was in jail but also because he was uninvited.

Group therapy sessions are also valuable because they give recovering persons an opportunity to learn how to recognize and avoid situations that trigger their drinking. Through group discussions, recovering alcoholics learn how their behaviors revolve around drinking, and how drinking revolves around certain behaviors. With this understanding, it is possible to avoid situations that might rekindle drinking.

Finally, group therapy provides a logical transition into the group fellowship of AA. The group meetings are very important to maintaining sobriety.

Betty, for example, was a charming, healthy woman who was deeply involved in charitable work for her church. When her husband of forty years died unexpectedly, her life seemed to crumble. She resented his untimely death, and she was lonely. At first she drank only wine at bedtime to sleep soundly. But alcohol overtook her, and she was soon hooked. Fortunately for Betty, she was guided into the eye-opening group meetings of AA. She recovered completely, and she resumed her charitable service work with eagerness and determination.

Some stories end less positively. Frank had been in recovery for fifteen years. But when he was fifty-four, he lost personal control to riverboat gambling, and eventually he started drinking again too. Frank stubbornly refused support from AA or any other treatment program. He was found dead in a motel room.

Alcoholics Anonymous and the Twelve-Step Program

Twelve-step therapy begins with individual and group counseling. Trained staff members help recovering persons and their family members understand how attending AA and Al-Anon meetings, while working AA's twelve-step program, can restore sanity to their lives and prevent relapse. Following is a modified version of AA's twelve steps (adapted from AA's Twelve Steps to Sobriety):

1. Alcoholics admit that they are powerless over alcohol.

2. They come to believe there is some greater power that can restore them to wellness.
3. They turn their will and their lives over to the care of the greater power, their God.
4. They make a searching moral inventory of themselves.
5. Recovering alcoholics admit to God, to themselves, and to other persons the nature of their wrongdoing.
6. They become ready to ask God to remove their shortcomings.
7. They ask God to remove their shortcomings.
8. They make a list of persons they have harmed and prepare to make amends to them.
9. They proceed to make apologies and reconcile with people on their list.
10. They learn to continually take personal inventories and admit when they are wrong.
11. They build conscious contact with God through prayer.
12. Having had a spiritual awakening as a result of following all the prior steps, recovering alcoholics carry their message to others with alcohol problems, and they practice the recovery principles in their daily lives.

The twelve-step approach of the AA program is a powerful way to achieve and maintain recovery. It is important for recovering alcoholics to stay involved in a strongly supportive group. Many are encouraged to set a goal for themselves: to attend ninety AA meetings in the first ninety days of recovery.

Individual therapy with an addiction professional helps the alcoholic and his or her family members understand each of the stages, use the program effectively, and become comfortable in the recovering community.

Long-term Relapse Prevention

The recovering alcoholic prevents drinking relapses by fully understanding alcoholism as a disease, following recommendations for proven treatments, recognizing the support and fellowship gained from participation in AA activities, and using the personal strength that comes from a strong faith in the power of God.

The following summary highlights key points from each of these aspects.

Understanding alcoholism
- Recognizing that alcoholism is a chronic, progressive illness that has specific symptoms and a predictable course.
- Realizing that persons with alcoholism have permanently lost the capacity to control their drinking.

Employing treatment strategies
- Recognizing that a single drink can trigger a craving that restarts compulsive drinking. A person with alcoholism must accept total, lifelong abstinence.
- Being aware that new medications are now available to help block alcoholic craving and break the vicious addiction cycle of craving and reward.

Drawing inspiration from AA groups
- Realizing that alcoholics have the best chance of staying sober over the long run if they accept their loss of control and reach out to fellow alcoholics through AA, using all its resources: meetings, hotline support, and personal sponsors.

- Listening to the many stories of lives rebuilt without alcohol, one day at a time.

Acknowledging the importance of spirituality
- Recognizing that alcoholism affects an alcoholic's body, mind, and spirit, and that true recovery requires healing in all of these dimensions, including the spiritual.
- Acknowledging that faith in God is stronger than individual willpower in maintaining sobriety.

Working hard to follow a well-planned program for recovery can help people successfully overcome the life-threatening disease of alcoholism. But the disease, once triggered, lasts a lifetime. It is important to remember that an AA program exists in virtually every community and is available whenever a recovering alcoholic needs it.

Here's an AA story with an unexpected ending. Kenny was an Oregonian with great passion for everything he did, but he was especially passionate about gardening. He was tireless in his efforts to achieve the perfect garden; his colorful and imaginative landscapes were the envy of the entire neighborhood. At one time, Kenny had a serious addiction to alcohol, but he was greatly helped by AA. He became such a firm believer in the AA program that he himself served as a sponsor for Tom, a newly recovering alcoholic. Kenny was doing well until he moved to a new home. He felt compelled to try to reconstruct the beautiful garden setting of his previous home and was disappointed when he could not achieve the desired effects right away. At this point, Kenny suffered a serious drinking relapse. It was Tom, the individual he was sponsoring, who convinced him to stop drinking and restart recovery.

Review the long-term prevention recommendations given on pp. 27-28. Are these "doable" and realistic?

Understanding Alcoholism and Its Implications

As you initially confront the complex nature of alcoholism — addiction, denial of addiction, withdrawal symptoms, behavior counseling, spiritual recovery, and relapse prevention — there will no doubt be aspects that are very confusing. Even as you read the next chapter explaining how and why alcoholism happens, you may be confused at first.

Consider then the advice of the Apostle Paul to his spiritual son Timothy: "Reflect on what I am saying, for the Lord will give you insight into all this" (2 Tim. 2:7). This message has two important parts. First, study is essential to comprehension, and second, divine illumination promises that you will eventually understand. Paul uses three images to explain how hard we must work to try to understand. We must work as hard as a soldier who supports the man who enlisted him, as an athlete who follows the rules of the contest, and as the farmer who produces the harvest crop.

In bullet form, make a list of what you already know about alcoholism. Now make a list of what you still need to find out about it. What will you do to get the answers you still need?

A Drugstore in the Brain
Dr. Doot Explains Alcoholism

How can a pastor become an alcoholic? Finding a way to answer this question weighed heavily on my mind the day I admitted Pastor DeJong to the alcoholism treatment program. The following Sunday I was scheduled to give a lecture about drinking to students at Trinity Christian College. Since many of these young people had been students or parishioners of Pastor DeJong, I knew they were searching for a logical answer to the question of how a good Christian, particularly a well-respected church leader, could become entrapped by alcoholism. I decided to try to answer this question by addressing two broader issues: Who gets alcoholism, and how does it develop?

Alcoholism: How It Happens

It is now recognized that nearly 15 percent of the adult population of the United States — at least 15 million people — actually meet diagnostic criteria for alcohol abuse or dependence during their lifetimes. It is also recognized that alcoholism ignores the boundaries of gender, age, race, eth-

31

nicity, and economic status. In short, ministers, mothers, monarchs, mechanics, and musicians — virtually anyone who consumes an alcoholic drink — can progress to alcoholism when certain conditions are present.

A Look Inside the Brain

To determine how a person "gets" alcoholism, let's first consider how alcohol affects the human body — particularly the brain. We clinicians and medical researchers can provide much better explanations today than we did at the time of Alex DeJong's diagnosis twenty years ago. Dramatic advances in medical science over the past two decades have, in fact, revolutionized our understanding of alcohol's complex effects, both inside and outside of brain cells. But to understand how alcohol works on the brain, we first need to understand how the brain itself works.

The brain is an intricate biological machine composed of billions of working parts called nerve cells or *neurons*. Neurons are cells responsible for complex functions such as reasoning, remembering, and reacting. Since brain neurons do not actually touch each other, they need somehow to communicate with each other for actions to occur. Neurons are thus wired to "talk" and "listen" to each other by way of branching extensions called *dendrites* and *axons* (see Figure 1A). Neuronal axons are activated by electrical impulses and "talk" by releasing chemical neurotransmitters from stored packets into the spaces between the cells. The transmitter chemicals move across the spaces, and dendrites "hear" signals when these chemicals fit precisely onto specific cell-surface receptors like pieces in a molecular jigsaw puzzle (see Figure 1B).

32

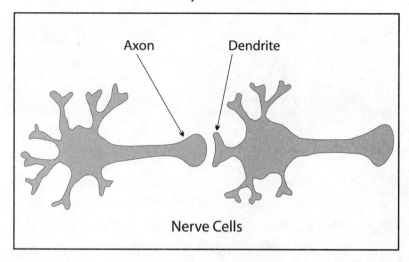

Figure 1A. Neurons are the working parts of the brain. Nerve cells or neurons in the brain "talk" and "listen" to each other by way of branching extensions called axons and dendrites.

Key to the brain's phenomenal function is the way it uses dozens of different chemical transmitters to call out specific responses among its billions of neurons. Through remarkable scientific advances, it is now known that when neurons in the "deep basement" of the brain are activated, each normally releases chemicals from the tips of its far-reaching axons. These chemicals bind to specific receptors on neurons in distant regions of the brain to elicit responses or feelings. While nearly a hundred chemical transmitters have now been identified, each neuron produces just one or sometimes a few different chemicals.

Brain researchers have recently been able to assign well-known feelings to specific brain chemicals and their receptors. In remarkable studies, scientists experimentally stimulated brain parts with electrical probes and with chemicals

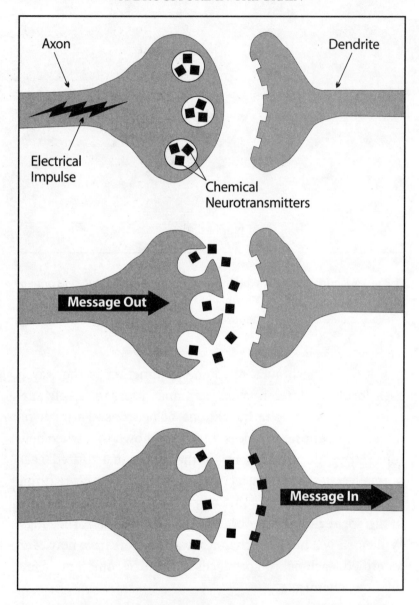

Figure 1B. Messages in the brain. Neuronal axons are activated by electrical impulses and "talk" by releasing chemical neurotransmitters. These chemicals move across spaces between cells and are "heard" when they bind to specific receptors on adjacent dendrites.

that mimic natural responses. The scientists thus identified roles for five such brain transmitters — glutamate, gamma aminobutyric acid (GABA), dopamine, beta-endorphins, and serotonin. In simple terms, glutamate acts as a neurochemical that increases alertness, gamma aminobutyric acid (GABA) induces feelings of peacefulness, dopamine elicits joy, beta-endorphins evoke pleasure, and serotonin produces patience (Figure 2, top).

Brain chemicals influence feelings

Brain chemical	Feeling
Glutamate	Alertness
GABA	Peace
Dopamine	Joy
Beta-endorphins	Pleasure
Serotonin	Patience

Another aspect of the brain's extraordinary functioning is the way that the billions of neurons are coordinated to work together. Using its chemical language, a single neuron can communicate with as many as 50,000 other neurons. All together there are about 50 trillion different ways that brain cells can possibly link with one another — enough "hook-ups" to enable us to perform the intricate tasks required for human survival, from breathing and being able to distinguish hot from cold to choosing between right and wrong.

35

A specific sequence of one neuron communicating with the next — a firing sequence — becomes the basis for specific actions or responses. For example, smelling the fragrance of roses relies on the patterned firing of specific neurons that are linked by specific transmitters. If the sequence is repeated — frequently smelling the roses in grandma's garden — then the firing sequence occurs more readily and is remembered. Even a rose-scented bathroom mist can elicit memories of the garden.

From Roses to Alcohol

So how does alcohol fit into this picture? How does alcohol affect the brain? Compared to other things we eat or drink, alcohol is composed of very small molecules. Because of their small size, alcohol molecules move quickly through the digestive system and are carried by the bloodstream to the brain. Alcohol molecules also readily dissolve in cell membranes. Alcohol thus sneaks up on the brain and hits neurons as if it were a well-stocked drugstore — alcohol simultaneously elicits brain responses that can also be produced by taking Valium, cocaine, morphine, and Prozac.

Medical discoveries over the past decade have revealed that alcohol provokes its wide range of mind-altering results by wreaking havoc with normal chemical signals in the brain. Alcohol interferes with glutamate, GABA, dopamine, beta-endorphins, and serotonin to produce effects long recognized in persons who have been drinking — slowed reaction times, relief of anxiety, boisterousness, bliss, sleepiness, and sometimes addiction and craving. Simply stated, alertness is lowered, while feelings of joy, peace, pleasure, and patience are elevated (Figure 2, bottom).

36

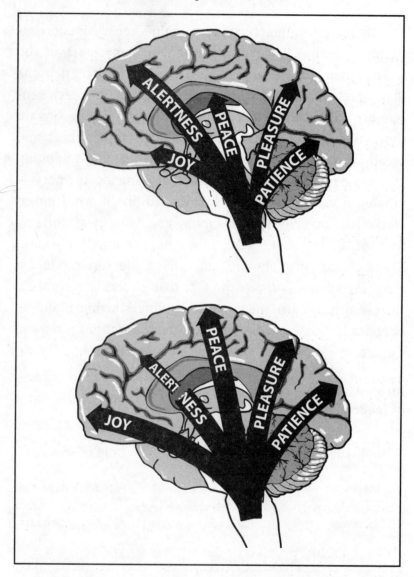

Figure 2 (top) Human feelings in the normal brain. Feelings of joy, alertness, peace, pleasure, and patience have each been related to release of specific chemicals in the brain. (bottom) Effects of alcohol on the brain. When a person drinks alcohol, levels of brain chemicals are altered. Alertness is diminished, while joy, peace, pleasure, and patience are elevated.

By inhibiting glutamate, the brain's most common excitatory chemical, alcohol slows down many parts of the brain. When alcohol inhibits glutamate's effects on neurons that control muscles, coordination is lost. When speech neurons are impaired, slurring results. If the affected neurons are those that regulate vital functions such as heartbeat and breathing, severe suppression can lead to death. By inhibiting glutamate receptor function, alcohol also impairs memory — ranging from cocktail-party ditziness to full-blown drunken blackouts. Such physically disabling and memory-stealing effects of alcohol have tremendous implications for health. These effects certainly don't describe a pleasure-producing drug. People drink *despite* the fact that alcohol can threaten their health and turn them into stumbling, slurring, brainless boneheads. So we need to look to other neurotransmitters to explain why a drink of alcohol is so compelling.

Alcohol and drugs override normal control of feelings in the brain

Brain chemical	Feeling	Drug effectors
GABA	Peace	Alcohol, Valium
Dopamine	Joy	Alcohol, cocaine
Beta-endorphins	Pleasure	Alcohol, morphine

Why Do People Drink?
Because Alcohol Reduces Anxiety.

While alcohol slows brain responses by blocking the ability of glutamate to elicit alertness, it also enhances the brain's normal braking system — the binding of gamma aminobutyric (GABA) molecules to their receptors. This is a desired effect because it reduces anxiety, an unpleasant feeling associated with a unique array of brain regions and chemicals. So alcohol, like the famed tranquilizer Valium, eases anxiety by enhancing GABA's "cool it" function to give drinkers a sense of peace.

Why Do People Drink?
Because Alcohol Elicits Joy and Pleasure.

Alcohol's duplicitous effects on the brain don't stop there. Within the last ten years, researchers have discovered that alcohol consumption is linked with the reward center of the brain by a chemical known as dopamine. Dopamine elicits a blissful state in a central region of the brain recognized as the *pleasure center.* Dopamine is likely a big part of the reason that persons with alcoholism have difficulty kicking their drinking habit. Medical researchers have found the sensation of pleasure to be highly compelling. They initially observed that rats wired to jolt themselves in this pleasure center would press a pedal for an electronic "fix" rather than eat, even in the face of starvation. Like these carefully placed electrodes and the street drug cocaine, alcohol acts quickly on dopamine receptors to stimulate the pleasure center of the brain. The cocaine-like "high" of alcohol is evidenced by feelings of excitement and rowdiness and even the sexual arousal that drinkers seek.

Direct evidence now indicates that dopamine activity plays a part in alcoholism. Recent scientific investigations have for the first time captured brain images of people who are in the throes of drinking and craving alcohol. Such studies indicate that alcohol — like amphetamines, heroin, and nicotine — markedly enhances the activity of dopamine receptors. Other breakthrough studies have revealed a familial form of alcoholism associated with inefficient dopamine signaling, which is due to a deficiency in dopamine receptors. Individuals with this deficiency presumably drink alcohol to simulate normal pleasure levels.

Why Do People Drink?
Because Alcohol Reduces Pain.

Alcohol also stimulates the action of beta-endorphins — the group of brain chemicals renowned for producing runner's "high." Since beta-endorphins act, in part, by boosting dopamine levels in the brain, the pleasure center gets a double whammy. Recent significant clinical discoveries showed that persons with a genetic vulnerability to alcoholism were deficient in beta-endorphins. Since such persons sensed a greater than normal beta-endorphin "rush" in response to alcohol, the pleasure of drinking was reinforced. Also, endorphins, like the notorious drug morphine, function as natural pain-killers, and thus further reinforce the pleasure of alcohol use. As pain decreases, pleasure increases.

Why Do People Drink?
Because Alcohol Contributes to Feelings of Well-being.

Serotonin, a brain chemical that staves off depression, is also implicated as a target of alcohol's effects. I have identified serotonin as the transmitter of patience, which allows us to face life's problems without getting depressed. Medical researchers investigated the role of serotonin in alcoholism, and they found that levels of this neurotransmitter were abnormally low in many alcohol-dependent patients. New studies have reported that Prozac, the antidepressant drug that elevates natural serotonin levels, reduced alcohol intake in such individuals, though the drug's effects were modest. These findings suggest that serotonin contributes to overall feelings of well-being — the feelings that are enhanced by alcohol consumption.

> How do you know if you're predisposed to becoming an alcoholic?

How Dependence Deepens

Our journey through the jungle of brain chemicals now brings us back to the familiar fragrance of grandma's rose garden. When a person drinks alcohol and repeatedly experiences less anxiety and more pleasure, the pathways responsible for the pleasurable reaction in the brain are remembered. Pleasure-seeking eventually drives the cycle until any lack of pleasure causes the drinker to crave the sensation. This cycle leads to the craving for alcohol.

Developing Tolerance

Repeated drinking changes the chemistry of the brain as well as its circuits. The nerve cells adapt to excessive amounts of alcohol, and the natural chemicals that alcohol stimulates can become depleted. When this happens, an individual shifts from drinking to feel pleasure to needing a drink to avoid physical cravings and feelings of anxiety and depression. The individual loses "patience" and, with it, self-control. This repeated cycle can actually fuel depression, one of the very things the drinker is trying to avoid.

Physical Withdrawal

A strong indicator of deepening dependence on alcohol is extreme physical dependence: to avoid uncomfortable symptoms, the individual must have alcohol in his or her system at all times. Without it, the hands shake, the heart races, blood pressure rises, the body perspires, and the mind races. Serious withdrawal can lead to convulsions, delusions, and even death. Withdrawal is the most powerful motivator of continued drinking or drug use and a sign of later-stage addiction.

The Power of Addiction

The fact that imprinted brain circuits link drinking with pleasure (or at least the absence of discomfort) also explains why persons recovering from alcohol dependence can so quickly relapse when they have a drinking "slip." Recovering drinkers who relapse don't start at the level of a beginning drinker but instead come back at the level of desperate drinking that drove them to seek sobriety in the first place.

Imprinted neurological circuits in the brain are responsible for the powerful forces of addiction. I recall a particularly poignant example of the cunning nature of relapse. After an extended bout of heavy drinking, Al achieved and maintained sobriety for many years. With his wife, he raised two sons, participated in church and community affairs, and held a good job. Then, for an unknown reason, he fell back into a pattern of heavy drinking. His marriage disintegrated, and his sons left home. Eventually he was found dead in a bedroom. Some people like Al become so deeply addicted that they are difficult to help. There is still hope for such individuals, but we have learned that interventions should take place as soon as relapse drinking becomes evident.

The Disease of Alcoholism

At this point we can review why some people are particularly vulnerable to alcohol addiction. According to the latest scientific evidence, it now appears that specific defects in normal signaling systems of the brain may form the basis for an inherited vulnerability to alcoholism. We have discussed deficiencies in the function of brain chemicals, including dopamine, beta-endorphins, and serotonin — all chemicals that lead to feelings of joy, pleasure, patience, and even bliss. Persons who respond to drinking alcohol with higher than normal sensations of pleasure are prone to addiction because of the predictable effects of reinforcement on the brain. Other persons who actually have deficiencies in natural pathways for producing pleasurable sensations may begin drinking alcohol just to feel normal; with continued drinking, they too become hooked.

The net result of these recent and remarkable medical advances is that we now recognize alcoholism as a disease of the brain. The disease is often characterized by specific brain deficiencies underlying the drinking behaviors. We also know that the pleasure patterns imprinted by prolonged, reinforced effects of alcohol on the brain are never lost. As a chronic disease, alcoholism is not curable, but it is treatable — and is thus similar to other chronic diseases like diabetes and high blood pressure. Like persons with these well-known disorders, those with alcoholism must be continuously monitored for wellness. Because of the nature of alcohol addiction, alcoholics may experience relapses. These too are treatable.

What should you do when you suspect that a friend or family member has relapsed into alcohol dependency?

Hope for Alcoholics and Their Families

Such extraordinary insights into the nature of alcoholism now provide more hope than ever for treatment of this disease. It now appears that alcoholism is not a single disorder with a single underlying defect, but likely occurs differently in different individuals. The common theme, however, is that all persons with alcoholism *already have* or *develop* brain defects that affect their pleasure centers.

Help from Therapeutic Drugs

Within the last five years, medical researchers have made remarkable strides in identifying therapeutic drugs that effectively address specific deficits or malfunctions. The drug *naltrexone* was the first of these targeted agents to be approved in the United States for prevention of relapse drinking. By blocking neuronal receptor sites that normally bind endorphins, naltrexone is thought to prevent the rewarding "rush" associated with drinking alcohol. *Acamprosate,* a drug with a chemical structure similar to GABA, has been used successfully in Europe and the U.K. to help maintain abstinence in recovering alcoholics. While its exact mechanism of action is not fully understood, acomprosate may lessen anxiety and lower craving to reduce the likelihood of relapse drinking. Studies testing a dopamine-like agent, *bromocriptine,* showed that it is mildly helpful in overcoming craving and anxiety in recovering alcoholics, although improvement was greatest in alcoholics who were identified as having particular defects in their receptors for dopamine. Likewise, antidepressant agents that act by increasing levels of serotonin — for example, *Prozac* — were found to be most effective for increasing abstinence in recovering alcoholics who also had depressive disorders. Taken together, these latter findings suggest that some day targeted therapies may be available for people identified as having particular types of alcoholism. We can also now envision using combinations of different drugs that could produce exciting therapeutic benefits.

Help from Positive Behaviors

Finding Natural Ways to Feel Good

Brain chemical	Feeling	Drug effectors	Natural effectors
GABA	Peace	Alcohol, Valium	Spirituality
Dopamine	Joy	Alcohol, cocaine	Friendships, accomplishments
Beta-endorphins	Pleasure	Alcohol, morphine	Exercise, sleep
Serotonin	Patience	Alcohol, Prozac	Stress control, eating well

Another way to recover from alcohol dependence is to embrace behaviors that produce natural increases in brain chemicals associated with feelings of pleasure and well-being. Exercise as well as sleep are now known to elevate levels of beta-endorphins, a natural means to pleasure. Eating healthy, regular meals promotes regular production of serotonin, the brain chemical known to control impulsive behaviors. Accomplishments in work as well as in sports and hobbies can provide pleasure to some people, no doubt due to a blend of brain chemicals that result in a sense of well-being. There is also no doubt that loving relationships with family members and friends can promote recovery and prevent relapses for alcoholics.

Strength from a Higher Power

From my observations, one of the most powerful influences on my recovering patients is *spirituality*. There is a personal peace, an inner strength, and a resolve to make the next day better that people who know the grace of God can feel. As a Christian physician, I believe that we are each loved by our Lord, who is patient and forgiving. The power of His love can be harnessed within us to overcome illnesses and life problems — even alcoholism.

On these last few pages, we find suggestions for how to gain pleasure, joy, peace, and patience in healthy ways. Do these work? Can you suggest others?

If alcoholism is so widespread, how should churches, families, and individuals address the issue?

Life in Recovery
Pastor DeJong Finishes the Story

Sobriety is a gift. When I returned home from treatment, I worked with this gift, and recovery from alcoholism became increasingly possible over time. I now understand that God was with me when Dr. Doot challenged me in his office: "Doc, in college you taught me what it means to believe and trust in God. Now it's time for you to put your trust in the Lord. I have an open bed for you. It's time for you to get a fresh start." With that moment, God gave me the gift of a first step toward sobriety. With that step came a chance for a new beginning.

The Hard Work of Entering Recovery

Every morning after I returned home from the hospital's alcoholism center, I went to my desk to chronicle the steps of recovery in my journal. Out of that journal came my first book, *Help and Hope for the Alcoholic*. After the book was published, I received a phone call. Bob, a high-school friend who was himself recovering from alcoholism, said to me, "The most important thing you wrote was on page 64. You wrote that hitting bottom and surrendering is a *gift*, that each person's bottom is different, but that all are occasions to receive God's gift of caring. In His own way and on His own schedule, God gives this gift to each of us."

Bob added, "I waited a long time for the gift of surrender to AA, and you waited a long time for the gift of accepting treatment in a recovery center. Thank you for sharing your experiences and feelings. Let's talk often — we need each other." I have never forgotten this call from Bob, and to this day we remain in touch with each other. Like Bob, I too am thankful. I thank God for the gift of surrender, I thank God for the gift of sobriety, and I thank God for full recovery without relapse.

Since the publication of my first book, I have worked with many people who were addicted to alcohol. Some have fully recovered from their addiction; others have had difficult relapses. All are in God's hands, and their addictions will be healed according to His wise and loving ways. People who want to recover can find the needed reassurance and support in the hands and heart of their God. God's gift of surrender is available to every suffering alcoholic. God has no favorites in the alcoholic community.

An inspiring story of surrender comes from George. Under the direction of a professional counselor, George's family intervened and enrolled him in a treatment program. George received God's gift of surrender and acknowledged God's call when he yielded to his intervening family members and humbly said, "Thank you for hearing my cry for help."

George entered treatment and began living one day at a time in those difficult early days of recovery. While in recovery, George shared with me a favorite version of the Serenity Prayer, originally written by Reinhold Niebuhr:

God, grant me the serenity
To accept the things I cannot change,
The courage to change the things I can,
And the wisdom to know the difference.
Living one day at a time,
Enjoying one moment at a time,
Accepting hardship as the gateway to peace.
Taking, as He did, the world as it is,
And not as I would have it.
Trusting that He will make all things right
If I surrender to His will.
That I may be reasonably happy in this life
And supremely happy with Him forever in the next.

How can "People who want to recover find the needed assurance and support in the hands and heart of their God" (p. 49)?

What is "God's gift of surrender" (p. 49)? How does it work?

Moving Forward in Recovery

Receiving God's Grace

As we overcame our addiction to alcohol, Bob, George, and I — with other recovering Christians — developed a special understanding of Ephesians 2:8: "For it is by grace you have been saved, through faith — and this not from yourselves, it is the gift of God — not by works, so that no one can boast." Our understanding of these Pauline words has three parts: (1) God's offered gift of surrender, (2) our acceptance of that gift, and (3) our feelings of gratitude for the sobriety that follows.

First, God willingly gives the gift of surrender to persons who lose the power to control their desire for alcohol and to manage their lives. God is under no obligation to give this gift. Neither the frequency nor the sincerity of our prayers obligates God to respond. God's gifts are given freely, graciously, and compassionately. That's the way God is!

Second, we must freely accept God's gift. For a gift to be fully accepted, it must be used. Accepting and using the gift of surrender establishes a relationship between God as giver and the alcoholics as receivers. God's presence empowers us to receive his gift of surrender and actively work toward lasting sobriety. Through God, we ask and we receive. We pray and we work.

Third, God's gift, accepted and used, generates a spirit of thankfulness. Gratitude is the air that I breathed when I returned home from the hospital to resume my pastoral work. Feelings of gratitude actually helped me overcome my intense fear of facing people who I assumed would be critical and disapproving.

Facing the Realities of Recovery

Consider the paradox of recovery. On the one hand, viewing alcoholism as an illness implies passiveness. Alcoholism is something that happens to me. On the other hand, the fact that alcoholism happens outside of my control zones means that it does not paralyze me. This blend of passiveness and activity defies logical analysis, but calls for perseverance and faith in God's unfailing love for people. This applies to both those sick with alcoholism and those healthy and drug-free.

> What do you think DeJong means when he says, "The fact that alcoholism happens outside of my control zones means that it does not paralyze me"?

Even though the Gospel says, "Fear not," I was surprised to discover firsthand that I had to work to overcome my fears. But I gradually learned the true meaning of these words. After my discharge from the alcohol treatment center, I was terrified by the thought of standing before my congregation and preaching for the first time. At the comeback service, however, I was surprised by how the elders of my church supported me. When the service concluded, these eight elders lined the center aisle, and each in turn shook my hand as I made the long walk past the pews of five hundred seated worshippers. With this gesture, they welcomed me back, let me know they were on my side, and reassured me of my role in the public ministry. I will long remember those encouraging handshakes, and I will long remember the wonder and gratitude I felt when members of the congregation followed suit.

The support I received from the church elders reminds me of a story from the New Testament. Mark, in his second chapter, tells of four men carrying a paralyzed friend to Jesus for help. Because Jesus was in a house and surrounded by a crowd, the men couldn't get their friend anywhere near Jesus. Eventually the men carried their friend to the flat rooftop of the house, opened a section of it, and lowered him into the presence of Jesus — they found a way to help. These four friends, like my own parishioners, were burden-carriers. The story concretely illustrates Paul's words in Galatians 6:2: "Carry each other's burdens, and in this way you will fulfill the law of Christ."

Support can come from caring family members, from church friends, from new friends, and sometimes from compassionate strangers. All of us recovering from alcoholism can experience the same kindness and caring that filled me with wonder and gratitude in those first difficult days of recovery. It was these gestures that helped me through the tough times.

The next major occasion I feared was a meeting of our church denomination leaders in Grand Rapids, Michigan. I didn't want to face these colleagues because I worried that my peers might regard me as a professional failure, a moral wreck, or an exposed hypocrite. But with prodding from my wife, Joanne, I reluctantly agreed to attend the meeting.

I went to the meeting fortified by the words of Jesus. Of a sinful woman, He said, "Therefore, I tell you, her many sins have been forgiven — for she loved much. But he who has been forgiven little loves little" (Luke 7:47). I was again surprised that my peers, like my church elders and my parish members, accepted and sincerely supported me.

Sustaining Recovery: Community Support

God's gift of surrender is the starting point for overcoming alcoholism. But the new life that follows does not develop in individuals in isolation — it grows in each of us as members of a community of recovering persons. This community is hard to imagine, but it became very real to Joanne and me when we joined other hurting people at outpatient recovery sessions sponsored by MacNeal Memorial Hospital. In these sessions, we learned that healing can happen in one-on-one sessions, in small groups of two, and in large-group experiences. We developed trust and friendships with people like Jim, Wes, and George and their wives. Our ability to move forward was enhanced as our camaraderie deepened; we all worked together to recover.

Group members strengthened and encouraged each other to undertake the twelve steps of the AA program. As we worked to find spirituality in recovery, it felt more like we were on a battleground than a playground. (I had a hard time because my religious comfort always rested more easily in doctrinal and church confessional concepts rather than in the sovereign and unpredictable ways in which the Holy Spirit often works.) We struggled together. We explored each other's dark sides in order to see light, and we faced each other's fearful sides in order to regain trust. We shared our stories and challenged each other to move forward to serene sobriety.

Eventually we progressed so that we actively sought spirituality along with sobriety. In these small Al-Anon and AA meetings, we talked about prayer, and we prayed together. As a group, we asked for God's help, and we helped each other find God. We discussed our twelve-step work as we reached out to help each other and to help others. In this way my recovery was strengthened by group work.

Guidelines for Recovery:
The Twelve-Step Program

We discovered that the twelve steps to recovery offered by the AA program are firmly based in spirituality. Gradually building faith in and dependence on God fortifies recovery from alcoholism. As recovering alcoholics, these are the steps we took together:

1. We admitted that we are powerless over alcohol — that our lives had become unmanageable.
2. We came to believe that a power greater than ourselves could restore us to sanity.
3. We made a decision to turn our will and our lives over to the care of God, *as we understood him.*
4. We made a searching and fearless moral inventory of ourselves.
5. We admitted to God, to ourselves, and to another human being the exact nature of our wrongs.
6. We were entirely ready to have God remove all these defects of character.
7. We humbly asked Him to remove our shortcomings.
8. We made a list of all persons we had harmed, and became willing to make amends to them all.
9. We made direct amends to such people whenever possible, except when to do so would injure them or others.
10. We continued to take personal inventory, and when we were wrong, promptly admitted it.
11. We sought through prayer and meditation to improve our conscious contact with God, *as we understood Him,*

praying only for knowledge of His will for us and the power to carry that out.

12. Having had a spiritual awakening as a result of these steps, we tried to carry this message to alcoholics and to practice these principles in all our affairs.*

The Bible: A Resource for Recovery

Whenever I read God's Bible, I think of Mary, the mother of Jesus, who said to Gabriel, God's messenger, "May it be to me as you have said" (Luke 1:38). The amazing powers of Jesus evident in His public ministry are rooted in the Holy Spirit, the power of the Most High, who overshadowed Mary as she conceived the Savior.

The Bible is God's inspired word, and God's Spirit makes the words of the Bible personally effective for each recovering person. The Bible serves as a rich resource for those of us who seek support for change. As a group of persons in recovery, we sought guidance from the text of the Bible, and we shared readings from the Bible. Listed on the pages following are several passages that helped us heal (all passages are quoted from the NIV).

*The Twelve Steps are reprinted and adapted with permission of Alcoholics Anonymous World Services, Inc. Permission to reprint and adapt this material does not mean that AA has reviewed or approved the contents of this publication, nor that AA agrees with the views expressed herein. AA is a program of recovery from alcoholism — use of The Twelve Steps in connection with programs and activities which are patterned after AA, but which address other problems, does not imply otherwise.

AA STEP	BIBLE VERSE
1. Recognizing personal weakness	The Lord said, "My grace is sufficient for you, for my power is made perfect in weakness." The disciple Paul replied, "That is why, for Christ's sake, I delight in weaknesses, in insults, in hardships, in persecutions, in difficulties. For when I am weak, then I am strong." 2 Corinthians 12:9, 10
2. Acknowledging strength from belief in God	When the disciples asked, "Why can't we cure this person?", Jesus replied, "Because you have so little faith. I tell you the truth. If you have faith as small as a mustard seed, you can say to this mountain, 'Move from here to there' and it will move. Nothing will be impossible for you." Matthew 17:19, 20
3. Accepting God's caring love	"Humble yourselves, therefore, under God's mighty hand, that he may lift you up in due time. Cast all your anxiety on him, because he cares for you." 1 Peter 5:6-7
4. Assessing personal moral defects	"Who can discern his errors? Forgive my hidden faults. Keep your servant also from willful sins; may they not rule over me." Psalm 19:12-13

AA STEP	BIBLE VERSE
5. Fully admitting all wrongs	"Find out what pleases the Lord. Have nothing to do with the fruitless deeds of darkness, but rather expose them. For it is shameful even to mention what the disobedient do in secret." Ephesians 5:10-12
6. Becoming ready to change	"And do not grieve the Holy Spirit of God, with whom you were sealed for the day of redemption. Get rid of all bitterness, rage and anger, brawling and slander, along with every form of malice. Be kind and compassionate to one another, forgiving each other, just as in Christ God forgave you." Ephesians 4:30-32
7. Being willing to change	"Put off your old self.... Put on the new self, created to be like God in true righteousness and holiness." Ephesians 4:22, 24
8. Being ready to seek forgiveness from others (and from God)	"Clothe yourselves with compassion, kindness, humility, gentleness, and patience. Bear with each other and forgive whatever grievances you may have against one another.... And over all these virtues, put on love." Colossians 3:12-14

Reverend DeJong Finishes the Story

AA STEP	BIBLE VERSE
9. Asking for forgiveness	Peter asked, "Lord, how many times shall I forgive my brother when he sins against me? Up to seven times?" Jesus answered, "I tell you, not seven times, but seventy-seven times." Matthew 18:21, 22
10. Admitting freely to our sins	"Therefore confess your sins to each other and pray for each other so that you may be healed." James 5:16
11. Seeking strength from God to carry out His will	"I said to the Lord, 'You are my Lord; apart from you, I have no good thing.'" Psalm 16:2 "The prayer of a righteous man is powerful and effective." James 5:16
12. Pledging oneself to a life of helping others	"I needed clothes and you clothed me, I was sick and you looked after me, I was in prison and you came to visit me." Matthew 25:36 "Whoever loves God must also love his brother." 1 John 4:21

Ultimate Recovery

Helping Others

I frequently receive phone calls, including calls from locations across the country and around the world. These calls come from teachers, clergy persons, mothers, wives, sons, daughters, and friends far and near. All ask about my experiences in recovery, and how I might help them or their loved ones. For twenty years now, God has enabled me to humble myself, to rest my cares on Him, and to draw on my firsthand experiences with alcohol addiction to help others. I am pleased to serve God in this way — by speaking to individuals, by speaking at public meetings, and by speaking on television. I am also pleased to be able to write books like this one. This is my practice of the twelfth step.

A few years after I entered recovery, I was asked to serve on a committee that drafted guidelines for pastoral dealings with church members who became addicted to alcohol or other drugs. Both Dr. Doot and I recognize that our faith in Jesus Christ must work in our daily affairs. Accordingly, we have served together on the Board of Directors of the Calvary Rehabilitation Center in Phoenix, Arizona. We also worked together to found the New Leaf Resource Center in Lansing, Illinois. There have been an amazing number of opportunities for Dr. Doot and me to answer God's call and touch the lives of people who are addicted.

What are concrete ways in which family, friends, and fellow church members can support an alcoholic during recovery? Will involvement in AA continue to be necessary?

Feeling Humbled and Thankful

Humbled and thankful, I have seen God's love in new ways. I have walked with others through valleys of fear, shame, and hopelessness. Along the way, God has never given up on me. The words of Psalm 119 ring true to me: "It was good for me to be afflicted so that I might learn your decrees" (v. 71).

For me, the lines of a familiar hymn have become a daily prayer:

Breathe on me, breath of God
Fill me with life anew,
That I may love what thou dost love,
And do what Thou wouldst do.

Further Resources

For the latest research on alcoholism, contact

The National Institute on Alcohol Abuse and Alcoholism
National Institutes of Health
Willco Building, Suite 409
6000 Executive Boulevard
Bethesda, MD 20892-7003

phone: 301-443-3860
fax: 301-480-1726
website: http://www.niaaa.nih.com

For the latest research on drug addiction, contact

The National Institute on Drug Abuse
National Institutes of Health
Parklawn Building, Room 10-05
5600 Fishers Lane
Rockville, MD 20857

phone: 301-443-1124
24-hour information line: 1-888-644-6432
website: http://www.nida.nih.com

For information on how communities can organize to prevent these problems, contact

Join Together
441 Stuart Street
7th Floor
Boston, MA 02116

phone: 617-437-1500
fax: 617-437-9394
website: http://www.jointogether.org

For the latest information on treatment, contact

The American Society of Addiction Medicine
4601 North Park Avenue
Arcade Suite 101
Chevy Chase, MD 20815

phone: 301-656-3920
fax: 301-656-3815
website: http://www.asam.org

For comprehensive information on substance abuse prevention, contact

The National Clearinghouse for
  Alcohol and Drug Information
P.O. Box 2345
Rockville, MD 20847-2345

phone: 1-800-729-6686 or 301-468-2600
fax: 301-468-6433
website: http://www.health.org